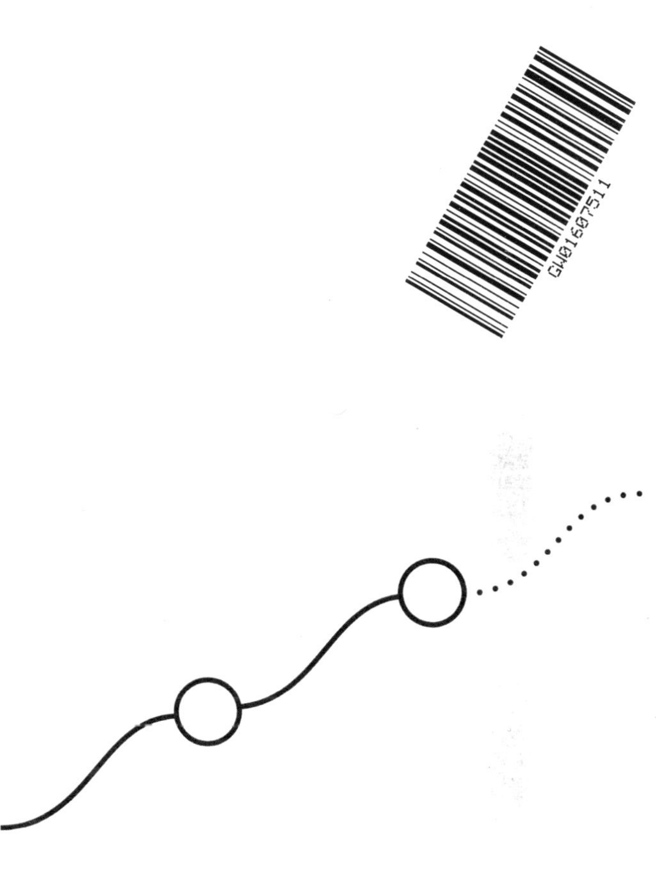

JESPER LOK
JIM HAGEMANN SNABE
MIKAEL TROLLE

REINVENTION FROM THE BOARDROOM

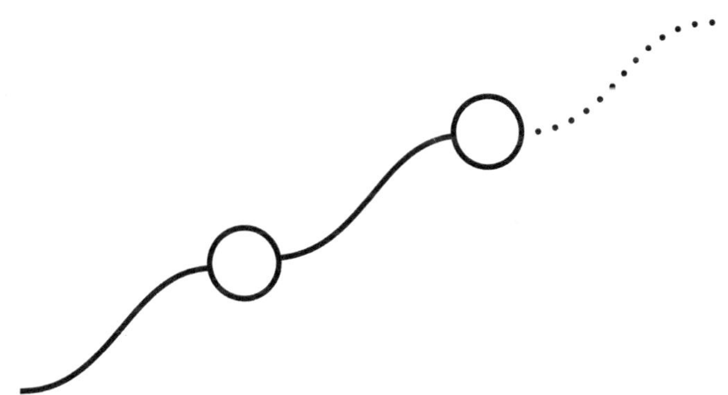

PRACTITIONERS' GUIDE
FOR BOARDS TO DRIVE
CONTINUOUS REINVENTION

spintype

"As a Board Chair and member of multiple boards, I've seen first hand how important boards are to the success of an organization. I've also seen how much has changed in the boardroom over the past several years, and how the best boards are able to embrace change and push beyond their traditional roles. Jim Snabe understands these dynamics better than anyone, and his book *Reinvention from the Boardroom* is a must-read for those who care about the role of businesses and leaders in a rapidly changing global landscape."

— Peter T. Grauer, Chairman, Bloomberg LP

"Against a backdrop of accelerating corporate change, this book explains why boards need to take steps to initiate transformation before it's too late. The authors provide thought-provoking suggestions on how this can be done, and questions to be asked to prepare businesses for a new environment. This is a useful guide for those looking to move from simple risk management to lasting resilience."

— Andreas Sohmen-Pao, Chairman BW Group

"For many years, we have been talking about what business can learn from sport. However, sports have just as much to learn from business. Especially on leading and driving innovative boards! This book is a tour de force in doing just that, and should be a companion to any board member or chair aiming to unleash the very best from their organizations."

— Kasper Hjulmand, National team coach, Football Denmark

Reinvention from the Boardroom
– Practitioners' Guide for Boards to Drive Continous Reinvention

1. Edition, 1. printing. 2022

Authors: Jesper Lok, Jim Hagemann Snabe & Mikael Trolle
Book layout: Spintype.com
Cover design: Per-Ole Lind, Spintype
Printed by: Ingram Spark
Published with: Spintype.com
Proofreader: ProofreadingPal

Isbn print: 9788771921397
Isbn pdf: 9788771921403
Isbn epub: 9788771921410

Join the dialog about leadership in a rapidly changing digital future:
www.idonea.dk

TABLE OF CONTENTS

Change happens so fast today that a company must be able to react long before it is obvious that it is necessary.

INTRODUCTION

RACES & SEASONS

When the book *Dreams & Details—Reinventing Your Business and Your Leadership from a Position of Strength* (Hagemann Snabe & Trolle) was published in 2017, we encouraged leaders to embrace a new leadership model and sought inspiration not merely from the business world but also from a range of other leadership settings including culture and sports.

A great source of inspiration was Ron Dennis, former chair of McLaren Technology Group, who has been involved in reinventing a number of industries based not least on his experience with Formula 1 racing. His ambitions and leadership philosophy are more relevant than ever. As he says, "The fact that you have won the Formula 1 World Championship many times in past seasons is no guarantee for winning it in the next season."

Within a Formula 1 season, the rules stay the same, allowing only for optimization of cars between each race to increase the chances of winning the next race. But between every season, the rules change, sometimes drastically, which forces participating teams to experiment with new technologies, design new cars and engines, rebuild the teams, and, above all, find innovative ways of working and performing.

Basically, you have to reinvent the company for each new season. If you continue to optimize the old car and the old team based on the old rules, you are already irrelevant at the first race in the new season.

This is exactly the dilemma all companies face: Should they risk reinventing themselves or risk not to?

In sports, it is easy to know when it is time for a new season: the development of the game, the rules, the schedule, the performance or lack of, speak for themselves.

It is crucial to identify whether it is sufficient to optimize or whether it is time to reinvent.

For a company, however, it is more difficult to know when the new season is emerging, but it is crucial for a company's survival to identify whether it is sufficient to optimize the existing business or whether it is time to reinvent it.

Most people agree that a change is imminent when results are not forthcoming or the company is losing money, but at that point it is often too late because the financial resources to explore new opportunities usually have already become limited.

The challenge is to reinvent the company for a new season while things are going well and the company is strong. Change happens so fast today that a company must be able to react long before it is obvious that it is necessary.

This booklet is about how boards can create value by contributing to the reinvention of the company and its leadership.

Jesper, Jim & Mikael

We are witnessing tectonic shifts
driven by disruption at an exponential pace
where speed beats size.

Chapter 1

IN A RADICALLY CHANGING WORLD . . .

. . . WE ARE WITNESSING TECTONIC SHIFTS . . .

The world is facing unprecedented change, not least in multiple fundamental infrastructure platforms.

We are, as the entrepreneur, thought leader, and author Tony Seba points out in several of his thought-provoking presentations, witnessing simultaneous disruptions in the fields of energy, transportation, materials, and information platforms that are bound to affect every industry.

At the same time, societal contracts are being fundamentally rewritten due not least to increased focus on sustainability, inclusion, and equity.

For the past 200 years, humankind has benefited from the Industrial Age. It has improved our standard of living radically and moved hundreds of millions of people out of poverty. Aside from occasional local wars, we have seen positive development on all populated continents, albeit at different speeds.

The Industrial Age is often characterized by the advent of mass production. Small, expensive, and slow handcraft production methods transitioned into standard products produced in large numbers in factories with the lowest marginal costs, often in countries with low wages. It pitted the local carpenter against IKEA and the local shipyard against an industrial facility like South Korean shipbuilder DSME.

Global standards have been a catalyst to boosting productivity.

Global standards have been a catalyst to boosting productivity. They have made it possible to sell to consumers globally and ship goods far at low costs, and it has created a global market competing on price.

Most of us have learned to lead based on the assumption that competitive advantage is created by producing goods on a mass scale as efficiently as possible—finding a continual balance between price and quality, where all aspects of the supply chain, from raw materials to the final product and logistics, must be optimized.

We often refer to the Industrial Age as a singular era, but in reality, it is more accurate to talk about "the industrial revolutions" because it has not been a smooth progression. Developments have happened in jumps when new technologies and production methods have created new opportunities for scale and optimization.

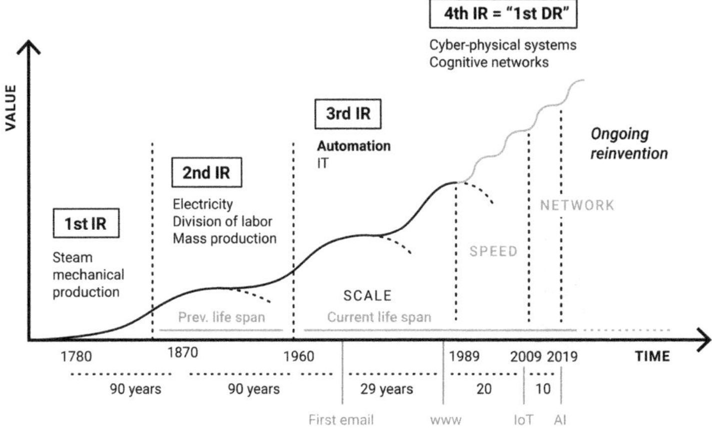

Figure 1 – The Industrial Revolutions
(IR: Industrial revolution, DR: Digital revolution, IoT: Internet of Things, AI: Artificial intelligence)

The improvements in efficiency and productivity in the first three industrial revolutions were driven by a series of trends enabled by technology:

- Specialization: Production and supply chains were divided into specific elements, which increased the possibilities for specialization and reduced costs. Individual companies and employees primarily focused on maximizing efficiency in their part of the value chain.

- Automation: The introduction of machines made specialized workforces even more efficient; production costs fell while real wages rose in the middle class, resulting in increased demand for mass products.
- Globalization: Standardization contributed to creating a wave of offshoring and outsourcing to countries where labor was cheap. Business models were developed based on producing at the lowest possible marginal cost.

Throughout the Industrial Age, the supporting logic has been economies of scale. This logic has created global giants, with size and scale as their competitive advantage. Being big has been an advantage, and the winning strategy has been to maximize the size and the scalability of the company and its market while minimizing costs.

Looking at the top Fortune 500 companies from the beginning of the 1960s to 1989, when the Berlin Wall fell and the World Wide Web was born, seven out of ten companies were the same: General Motors, Exxon Mobil, Ford Motor, General Electric, Chrysler, Texaco, and IBM.

Companies structured around economies of scale had, in other words, a sustainable competitive advantage for many decades.

If we look at the list of companies with the highest value from 1989 to today, it has changed radically. More than 60 percent of the most valuable companies today are digital companies, relatively young, with business models based on digital platforms—not mass-produced products.

More than 60 percent of the most valuable companies today are digital companies.

If we turn the clock back to 2008, Walmart had a market value of $210 billion, and the internet startup Amazon was worth $20 billion, or one-tenth of the value of Walmart. Only thirteen years later, in 2021, Walmart's market valuation was $400 billion. The retailer had a solid increase of its market value, 90 percent in total since 2008. Amazon, however, was worth $1.6 trillion, more than four times as much as Walmart at the end of 2021 and had become one of the most valuable companies in the world. Walmart's value had merely increased linearly, whereas Amazon's value followed an exponential curve, increasing by an astonishing 7,900 percent over the thirteen years. In the past four years alone, the value of Amazon had tripled.

In 2008, Walmart employees were probably not worried about Amazon. Today, it is difficult to imagine that Walmart will come back and take the lead over Amazon.

Today, nimble start-ups challenge century-old companies.

Today, nimble start-ups challenge century-old companies. Delivery platforms like Wolt are traded at EUR 7.5 billion just a few years after they were established, and Tesla is worth more than $1 trillion. Toyota in comparison is the second most valuable car company but worth less than a quarter of Tesla, and Daimler is worth merely $85 billion.

The only companies more valuable than Tesla are Apple, Microsoft, Alphabet (Google), and Amazon.

... DRIVEN BY DISRUPTION AT AN EXPONENTIAL PACE ...

So, what has changed? Globalization continues, as does the opportunity to maximize scale using new technology. Based on that logic, the same management models should still be viable.

In the meantime, a fourth industrial revolution, which is more likely the start of the Digital Age, has gained momentum and changed the logic. Whereas the other industrial revolutions have been mostly mechanical, this revolution is now highly digital.

Digitalization, in many cases, changes the linear curve to an exponential one because the technologies are interconnected through networks, thus constantly gaining new connection points and data while continuing doubling speed and capacity and reducing costs.

In other words, the logic that ruled the former three industrial revolutions is no longer relevant to the same degree. To stay relevant in the future companies have to increasingly recognize these key points:

- Segmentation is dead: Companies have long thought in terms of target groups and segments. But when we get the opportunity to meet our customers' individual needs, we do not need to think about the most lucrative target groups. Instead, we can focus on how to satisfy each customer individually. This is where technologies such as big data, artificial intelligence (AI), and the Internet of Things (IoT) are important because they enable us to understand the individual needs of customers and to interact with them directly.
- Platforms replace assets: Digital technology allows us to shift focus from a product's value to the exponential value of a platform. Airbnb is a good example. It does not own any rooms but is based on a digital platform that directly brings people with surplus room capacity together with people in need of a place to stay. The value is the platform itself, not the rooms, which differentiates the business model of Airbnb distinctly from that of a hotel chain,

even though the basic product—a place to stay away from home—is nearly the same.

- Service models win: Economies of scale are being replaced by economies of scope and the benefits of having a wide range and impact. We should not only optimize specific parts of the value chain but also reduce complexity and increase beneficial impact for the customer across the entire value chain. To give an example from the wind power industry, the company does not just sell a turbine to a customer and leave it at that. It remains in control of the turbine's operation and maintenance, and it harvests all the data from it and can thereby optimize its uptime and reduce maintenance costs. This provides a benefit for the customer and an opportunity for a larger share of wallet and profit margin for the company as well. The flood of data, used and analyzed correctly, also creates opportunities for innovation and improvements of services.

But the disruption we are facing is about more than digitalization. We are facing simultaneous disruption resulting also from increasing geopolitical uncertainty and the expanded sustainability agenda.

We might have talked about this for a long time, but we are now at inflection points. This necessitates that boards emphasize these important ideas:

Your organization is required to take active part in solving value chain challenges.

- As the geopolitical state of the world becomes increasingly uncertain, risk management becomes resilience management. It is no longer about knowing every risk but about creating resilient organizations who can deal with uncertainty as it arises.
- Sustainability is no longer about what you do as a company but how you impact and contribute to the entire value chain. Your organization is required to take active part in solving value chain challenges. The board is thus required to expand its perspective and take an active role in making sure the organization has the partnerships needed.
- Activists expect businesses—not governments—to act. The major push for change is no longer driven by legislation. Activists play an increasing role as a key stakeholder and may impact your business negatively if not considered and included.
- Consumer discourse drives all three. As the world becomes connected like never before, single consumers may spark a revolution in behavior. Lately, companies choosing to stay

operational in Russia during the war with Ukraine or even just reacting a little too late have lost consumer confidence and loyalty in a matter of days that had taken decades to develop.

- Multistakeholder orientation is the premise for operating any business today.

... WHERE SPEED BEATS SIZE.

Until a few years ago, digital technologies mainly disrupted industries where the physical products could be replaced by digital versions, such as music, film, media, money, and advertising. The winners were digital companies like Google, Facebook, Netflix, and Spotify that did not have the disadvantage of a relatively slow physical supply chain but could reinvent the industry based on digital assumptions.

Digital platforms transform business models.

The traditional assumption that a company needs to own its assets to create value is also being challenged by the digital business model. Uber, Airbnb, and a number of other digital platforms do not own assets. Even the new banking platforms do not have cash or branches. They just connect supply and demand directly and have changed the game for established companies.

Digital platforms transform business models. Old players that used to benefit from size and scale are overtaken by small but fast digital companies that know the individual customer better because of their access to customer data and utilization of online technologies to connect supply with demand, without any intermediary.

The exceptional feature of digital technology is that it challenges the traditional assumption of economies of scale. Instead, the competitive advantage is moved to the platform and the value of the data. Marginal costs and distribution costs of the platform are virtually zero. This means that the earlier Industrial Age logic, where competition focuses on scale to reduce marginal costs, is no longer sufficient.

Digitalization challenges the logic of standardization.

At the same time digitalization challenges the logic of standardization. Customers are not necessarily eager to consume standard products. They tend to buy standard products if they are cheaper, but most consumers would prefer a customized product if it were available at the same price.

Digitalization allows companies to understand consumer preferences more accurately and deliver on individual needs and preferences. Editor-in-chief of *Wired Magazine* Chris Anderson wrote the book *The Long Tail* about how digitalization strengthens individualism. The title of the book is inspired by a graph showing that the aggregated market for niche products far exceeds the market of the most popular products. Earlier phases of the Industrial Age favored mainstream products and bestsellers, but digitalization gives advantage to companies that can fulfill the customers' exact wishes.

And that is just the beginning.

This development has been on its way for decades but has now gained momentum and speed as digital technologies begin to deploy AI and become interconnected. Through the IoT, most physical products become digitized and connected. Through the addition of AI, physical products begin to learn, update, and maintain themselves, accelerating technological opportunities beyond anything we have ever seen before.

Chair and CEO of Softbank Masayoshi Son compares this digitalization with the biological phenomenon called the Cambrian Explosion more than 500 million years ago, when visual abilities changed our evolution. His 30-year-vision is a world where the artificial computer brain will have an intelligence quotient (IQ) of 10,000, compared with 100 for the average human. He also predicts that by 2040, there will be an army of 10 billion intelligent robots making human lives easier.

So opportunity has never been bigger or better, but there are also many challenges currently left unsolved. Changes in a specific field not only involve the product or the service that is the direct subject of change but the surrounding services and society at large. How do we, for instance, prepare for the advent of self-driving vehicles? Not only will they reinvent the automotive industry, the traditional car insurance market will also need to be reinvented—not to mention driving schools, the taxi industry, and gas stations. The need for parking spaces will diminish, as will the need for road capacity, potentially leading to significant changes in the fundamentals of the real estate industry as well as in city planning.

The same thought experiment is relevant in all industries.

What happens to the energy value chain when energy, such as Power-to-X, is extracted from renewable energy sources like sun, water, and wind at significantly lower cost than burning fossil fuels?

What happens to consumer product value chains and manufacturing when it is possible to produce individualized products close to the consumer? What happens if the customer can produce these products themselves through 3D printing?

What happens to health care systems when we move from curing to preventing?

The reinvention of the car, which became the symbol of the second industrial revolution and its assembly lines, illustrates just how comprehensive and different the Digital Age is.

It is poised to make a season change in all industries.

In such a world, the models and approaches to leadership are also bound to change. The competitive advantage is rather in the skills and capacities to imagine, innovate, and excel more so than in optimizing. In our books *Dreams & Details* and the upcoming *Unleashing Human Potential*, we touch upon the "to do" leadership model and the "to be" leadership approach, which will deliver better results under these new realities.

Changes are unsurprisingly also necessary in the boardroom, which is what the rest of the book is all about.

In such a world, the models and approaches to leadership are also bound to change.

The board must move beyond its traditional roles, insist on simultaneous performance and transformation, and cultivate brutal honesty and the right dynamics in the boardroom.

Chapter 2

THE BOARD NEEDS TO REINVENT ITSELF

THE BOARD MUST MOVE BEYOND ITS TRADITIONAL ROLES . . .

Historically, companies were owned by individuals, families, or small groups of partners.

However, in the middle of the eighteenth century, modern corporations emerged and allowed people to invest without getting actively involved in running the business or assuming personal liability.

More people started buying stocks, and companies were suddenly owned not just by a few but by hundreds or thousands of investors.

This development allowed companies to grow—but with size also came complexity.

Before the modern corporation, where owners and managers were often the same people, it was relatively easy for a small number of people to gather and exchange information. These people usually knew each other well and shared a bond of trust.

As the number of shareholders grew and as investors increasingly were not part of management, the need for governance and supervision increased.

When all shareholders were gathered to be informed and have their say, however, meetings often ended up being chaotic, with endless debate, conflicting ambitions, and, as a result, often a lack of meaningful decisions.

The annual general meeting was introduced as a way to handle that dilemma, but with that came the challenge that shareholders started feeling uneasy about only getting information once a year. And between those meetings, they were hearing rumors about the conduct of management. The board was installed, and, to ensure equal treatment of all shareholders, independent directors joined these boards.

Boards that consisted of members that were appointed by the shareholders to serve their interests were small enough to meet regularly and take the necessary decisions. Their main focus was governance and, of course, the financial wellbeing of the company, with the board protecting the economic interest of the shareholders.

For long decades this was sufficient. Although changes have always been a part of business life, they used to be fewer and slower.

To a large extent, it was possible to predict developments in the near future, and the board would usually pay more attention to whether the company lived up to promises and expectations than to opportunities in the future.

But as has become apparent and is becoming increasingly urgent and critical, boards need to focus on much more than governance.

Boards need to focus on much more than governance.

And yet, Wikipedia suggests this, even in 2022:

> Typical duties of boards of directors include:
>
> - governing the organization by establishing broad policies and setting out strategic objectives;
> - selecting, appointing, supporting and reviewing the performance of the chief executive;
> - terminating the chief executive;
> - ensuring the availability of adequate financial resources;
> - approving annual budgets;

- accounting to the stakeholders for the organization's performance;
- setting the salaries, compensation and benefits of senior management

But think about it. If boards were so dominantly about governance, the boardroom should soon be taken over by AI.

. . . INSIST ON SIMULTANEOUS PERFORMANCE AND TRANSFORMATION . . .

The challenge facing every board is the need to simultaneously:

- Perform: Protect the business and extract optimal value
- Transform: Create new value for the business and society

As Wikipedia indicates, boards have focused their attention toward oversight of performance more than transformation. And over the years, boards have been driven to focus on perfomance by an equally well-meaning corporate governance regulation, which most countries have formulated for listed companies and encouraged companies in general to adhere to. It comes therefore as no surprise that there is significant focus on "the rule book."

But as business cycles have shortened and cyclicality and unpredictability is on the rise, the importance of paying increased attention to transformation has become apparent.

In a 2021 report, the Danish business network for Resilient Governance, of which we are members, asked this crucial question: What makes it possible for some companies to transform again and again and for some to be agile even at the age of 100? In other words, how have these companies apparently been able to institutionalize resilience and reinvention?

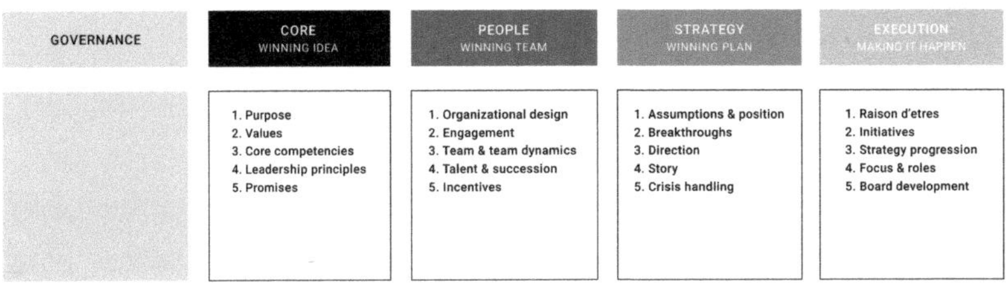

Figure 2 – Resilience Recommendations

In its report, the network points to four areas besides governance that are critical to building resilience: core, people, strategy, and execution. The report recommends that boards pay attention to and build the twenty disciplines that support resilience in these areas into their annual wheels, thereby creating agility.

In many ways *Dreams & Details* is the business model approach to building the resilient muscle. You stay in business and grow by focusing simultaneously on winning the races of the current season while preparing for the next season. Unless the business finds itself in significant crisis, the most important task the board has is to focus on reinventing your business from a position of strength. And even if it is in crisis, it must make sure time is spent on the transformation that will eventually be needed.

Making sure that time is spent on the transformation that will eventually be needed is imperative.

But why is it so hard to simultaneously perform and transform? Why is it so hard to build resilient organizations? Why is it so hard to reinvent businesses from a position of strength?

According to research by the global consulting firm Korn Ferry, less than 14 percent of executives have the "capabilities to both perform and transform, along with the capacity and agility to pivot dynamically between the two." We argue that lack of capabilities is due not least to using the wrong approach to strategy development. And Korn Ferry fortunately also concluded leaders can develop that capability through a new leadership approach, self-awareness, and personal growth and development.

In other words, it is possible to foster the mindset needed to flourish now and in the future; it is not something you either have or do not.

It will be increasingly important for board professionals to ensure that resilience and transformation are as high on the agenda as governance and performance and especially that members of the executive team develop the mindset needed to master both.

The German *Aufsichtsrat*, seems far more relevant than "board," which is merely reference to the historical fact that this group of people met around a table.

Aufsichtsrat comprises both *Aufsicht*, which is the oversight responsibility, and *rat*, which is the advice obligation.

Setting the ambition of being an "Aufsichtsrat," which could be translated into supervision council but also carries the meaning of "looking from above," makes it far more obvious that the task at hand is about a lot more than governance, and that it requires more insights, curiosity, and human understanding to be a board member in the Digital Age.

. . . AND CULTIVATE BRUTAL HONESTY AND THE RIGHT DYNAMICS IN THE BOARDROOM.

Boards rarely have the luxury of being in no-brainer or black-and-white situations. If something is the obvious choice, it is not really a choice at all, just an inevitable action. Most board work, apart from maybe the governance part, is, by definition, about navigating unpredictability and making choices, frequently difficult ones.

Decision-making in that space is particularly vulnerable to two types of pitfalls—derailers and biases.

One derailer is **escalating commitment**, which describes the "human behavior pattern in which an individual or group facing increasingly negative outcomes from a decision, action, or investment nevertheless continues the behavior instead of altering course."

Albert Einstein said it in a more direct way: "The definition of insanity is doing the same thing over and over and expecting different outcomes."

What led some companies such as Blockbuster, Barnes & Noble, and Kodak, to name a few, to ignore the realities facing their business models, while other companies, often start-ups like Apple, Amazon, Tesla, and Uber, just to name a few others, rose to historical highs?

Harvard Professor Clayton Christensen wrote about this phenomenon in his book *The Innovator's Dilemma,* explaining how most companies use all their resources to keep current customers satisfied and develop solutions for the most demanding of them.

According to Christensen, companies do not take competition from disruptive start-ups seriously, and he was not optimistic about companies' abilities to reinvent themselves because they tend to defend their historic positions instead of challenging them.

We suggest that Christensen's dilemma is due to the traditional leadership model of merely optimizing a successful business, with deteriorating performance and relevance as a consequence, instead of reinventing it from a position of strength.

There are many examples of companies reinventing themselves and changing seasons convincingly, but it requires leadership and guts to challenge your assumptions, the current success and begin a process of reinvention.

Just like we saw with the industrial and digital ages, the life cycle of a company usually follows what is called a sigmoid curve, named after the Greek letter Σ. A company is founded, grows, stagnates, declines, and eventually fades and dies or is taken over. As technological development accelerates, this cycle goes faster and faster, making the shelf life of companies shorter in recent decades.

A McKinsey study from 2016 pointed out that back in 1961 the average age of S&P companies was fifty-eight years. Just fifty-five years later, this had been reduced to eighteen years, and it was predicted that by 2027, 75 percent of those companies will also have disappeared.

By identifying a season change in time, a company can jump to the next sigmoid curve.

By identifying a season change in time, a company can jump to the next sigmoid curve to begin new developments with new opportunities rather than fade away. The optimal time to jump off the curve is when the company is at the top of the curve—before it really starts to decline. At this time it will have the financial strength and the credibility to do so. But it is crucial that the company does not adhere to the "if it ain't broken, don't fix it" doctrine.

When business cycles were longer and more predictable this mantra made much more sense. But in the Digital Age, the board needs to rephrase that mantra to "if it ain't broken, let's rethink it."

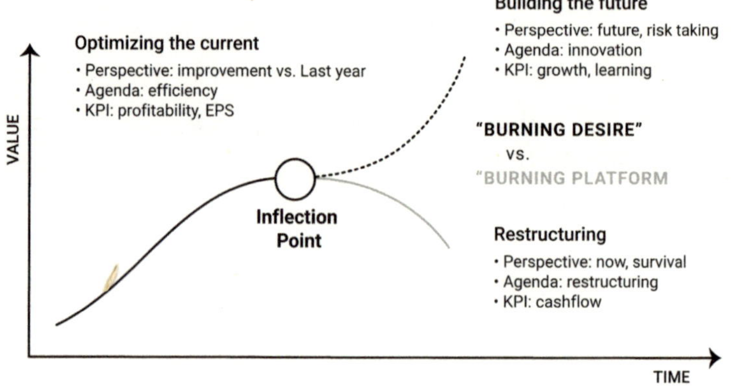

Figure 3 – Reinvention from a Position of Strength
(EPS: Earnings Per Share, KPI: Key Performance Indicators)

Companies that are good at reinventing themselves can move to the next season again and again. Exponential growth can be achieved by the optimal timing of these seasonal changes. Amazon is an interesting example—it went from being an early online bookstore to an e-commerce platform and on to being a cloud platform, leading the cloud computing season. Today, Amazon is a multifaceted physical and digital company that constantly develops new services and products.

It is essential that boards react to the early indicators of the need for transition rather than waiting until the revenue drop is happening. At that time, especially in a radically changing world, it might be too late.

In his book *Only the Paranoid Survive*, Andrew Grove, then CEO of Intel, explained a strategic inflection point as "a time in the life of a business when its fundamentals are about to change. That change can mean an opportunity to rise to new heights. But it may as likely signal the beginning of an end."

Grove suggested leaders should substitute escalating commitment with paranoia. If nothing seems to need fixing, then you probably have not looked hard enough.

Another derailer is **bureaucracy**.

Back in 1977 Professor Abraham Zaleznik described in a *Harvard Business Review* article entitled "Managers and Leaders: Are They Different?" what is likely to happen inside a company in the absence of strong leadership and clear priorities:

- First, the manager focuses attention on procedure rather than on substance.
- Second, the manager communicates ambiguously to avoid making a choice.
- Third, the manager plays for time.

When bureaucracy takes over, just like when excessive controls defy logic, the best people will eventually find better places to use their talent, and transformation will stall. It is not uncommon to confuse activity with meaningful action—sometimes it is even woven into individual key performance indicators (KPIs) that do not support performance. Bureaucracy with its diffusions exacerbates this tendency.

The other type of pitfalls is biases.

As the psychologist Daniel Kahnemann has shown in his research and books, biases can result in poor decision-making because our intuitions or systematic patterns of response frequently lead us astray.

The area has been well researched over the years by many psychologists who have come across ten to fifteen general cognitive biases. All can be detrimental to decision-making, however, some are particularly dangerous in the boardroom:

- Status quo
- Confirmation
- Groupthink

The **status quo bias** is about the tendency to hold on to the current situation rather than alternatives to avoid uncertainty, risk and loss.

American author and humorist Mark Twain said, "I'm in favor of progress; it's change I don't like." This sums up how most of us feel. Only by being conscious of that will we be able to overcome this instinct and help others to do likewise.

The **confirmation bias** is about the tendency to selectively search for and interpret information in a way that confirms one's preconceptions or hypotheses – or what we want to be true.

One of the challenges of search engines is that they are based on algorithms that prioritizes the information that is most likely to reinforce what you already have read before. It takes a real and conscious effort to get opposing views.

At a Bata board meeting, Thomas G. Bata (Tom), the then third-generation CEO of the Bata group founded in 1894 by his grandfather, asked one of the non-executive directors over dinner to share what had been the most surprising thing he had come across recently.

When asked how he had coined this fascinating question that forced everyone to scan for the unknown rather than search for signs confirming what was already known, Tom replied, "My father always asked that question."

Some good habits fortunately never die, and this is one worth bringing along.

The **groupthink bias** is about the tendency for people to give preferential treatment or consideration to others they perceive to be members of their own group, causing a tendency to agree at all costs—even when whatever is agreed upon could become catastrophic.

In decision-making in general, but in dealing with this bias in particular, one of the most effective debiasing tools is to invite and ensure diversity of thought.

This begins naturally with gender but should also include age, geography, background, history, social aspects, business, and faith, and particularly so in a world that is increasingly interconnected.

Diversity also is an effective catalyst to cultivate brutal honesty and the right dynamics.

Just think of the young child in Hans Christian Andersen's fairy tale "The Emperor's New Clothes." Only a child with no understanding of power, hierarchy, vanity, or consequences had the courage to say what everyone else knew—that the emperor was stark naked. Others did not like to say it out loud when they faced the emperor parading naked in the belief he was wearing the most exquisite fabrics money could buy.

Only a child had the courage to say what everyone else knew.

Boards need to ensure they have at least one or two such challengers as members around the table.

But it also takes a couple of other components to cultivate brutal honesty in the boardroom:

- Trust
- Candor

Trust cannot be commanded; it must be earned. But it is not nearly as fluffy as this might sound. In fact, we believe there is a pretty strong formula when it comes to trust.

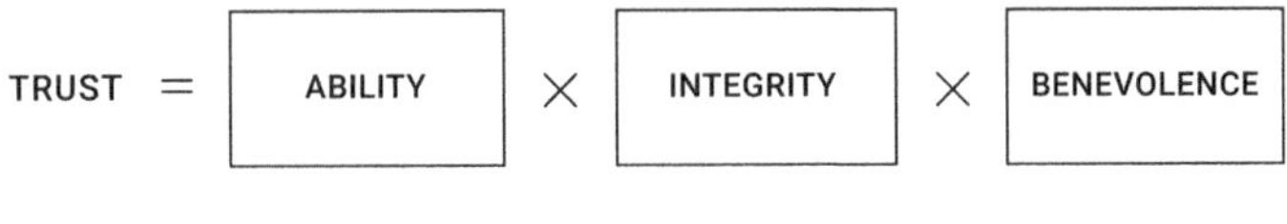

Figure 4 – Trust

Trust comprises three critical ingredients: ability, integrity, and benevolence.

In an increasingly digital and transparent world, it would be foolish to believe that you can get away with not being a role model of all three components.

It would be foolish to believe that you can get away with not being a role model of all three components of trust.

Yet some people seem to believe trust is merely the sum of these three ingredients, which might explain why some appear to believe that as long as you are capable, you can be a jerk.

Most people, however, have by now come to the realization that trust is the multiplication of the three, and failure on any of the components is simply not an option.

Those who still do not get this will continue to represent risks to the integrity of corporations, and they will fail as leaders to build a safe space for people to grow and businesses to transform.

To ensure the board comprises both ability and benevolence, it can be helpful to formulate a Competence Map.

Competence Map			Name	Name	Name	Name	Name	Name	Name	Name	Name	Strengths
Role												
Last appointment												
Member since												
Succession												
Industry Experience	This Season	-										
		-										
	Next Season	-										
		-										
Task / Role experience		CEO										
		C-Suite										
		Chair										
		NED										
		-										
		-										
		-										
		-										
Personal Attributes		Diplomat										
		Challenger										
		Comm. skills										
		-										
Diversity		Age										
		Gender										
		Geography										
		-										
		-										

Figure 5 – Competence Map

All boards need to ask themselves what the most important competencies to capture in the boardroom are. It is not enough that the board is comprised mainly by industry experience; it is equally important there are members with concrete insight into main risks and opportunities. And finally, it is important to recognize which specific experience and competencies as well as personal attributes that each member brings to the room.

The latter is important, not least to understanding whether the board is likely to exhibit the benevolence necessary to build trust. And the Competence Map is also helpful when keeping an eye on diversity and to ensure you walk the talk.

Trust in the boardroom is a prerequisite for building **candor** in discussions.

There can be a variety of reasons why candor has a hard time. A strong chair or CEO often makes candid conversations difficult. A lack of psychological safety is another reason why people will be calculated and cautious rather than candid.

All development begins with the recognition that things need to improve.

But candor is critical for any company to change and transform. All development begins with the recognition that things need to improve. And candor is the catalyst to getting there.

Netflix works systematically with candor. Erin Meyer's *No Rules,* which she coauthored with Reed Hastings, Netflix's cofounder and CEO, is a powerful description of its importance.

In the book, they refer to the 2014 study by the consulting firm Zenger Folkman, which collected feedback from almost 1,000 people. The study found that, despite the benefits of praise, people believe, by a roughly three-to-one margin, that corrective feedback does more to improve performance than positive feedback:

- 57 percent of respondents claimed they would prefer to receive corrective feedback to positive feedback.
- 72 percent felt their performance would improve if they received more corrective feedback.
- 92 percent agreed with the comment, "Negative feedback, if delivered appropriately, improves performance."

Surely all leaders and all business schools must be looking for and teaching insights into delivering appropriate feedback. This seems, however, not to be the case.

Netflix found it necessary to teach all employees to give and receive feedback well and thus tap into that 92-percent potential. It summarized this in its 4A guideline, phrased wonderfully informal and candidly in these points:

- Aim to assist: Feedback must be given with positive intent. Giving feedback to get frustration off your chest, intentionally hurting the other person, or furthering your political agenda is not tolerated. Clearly explain how a specific behavior change will help the individual or the company, not how it will help you.
- Actionable: Feedback must focus on what the recipient can do differently.
- Appreciate: The natural human inclination is to provide a defense or excuse when receiving criticism; we all reflexively seek to protect our egos and reputation. When you receive feedback, you need to fight this natural reaction and instead ask yourself, "How can I show appreciation for this feedback by listening carefully, considering the message with an open mind, and becoming neither defensive nor angry?"
- Accept or discard: You will receive lots of feedback from lots of people while at Netflix. You are required to listen and consider all feedback positively. You are not required to follow it. Say "Thank you" with sincerity. But both you and the provider must understand that the decision to react to feedback is entirely up to the recipient.

Another practical approach to cultivating candor is the "sun/cloud" matrix where long reports are replaced with a single slide with bullets outlining respectively what is working well and what requires further attention.

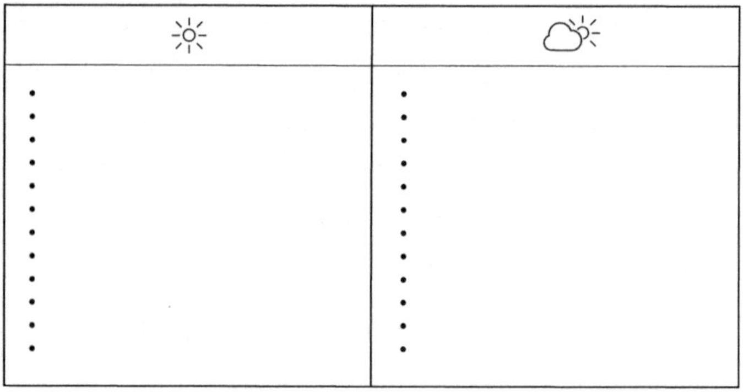

Figure 6 – Sun & Cloud

As simple as it is powerful, this chart provides an excellent background for real conversations and exchanges of insight.

For it to work, people must be able to bring up issues that might merely have been identified and not necessarily yet been solved.

Candor is not only relevant in the organization at large. It is also of vital importance in the boardroom to conquer biases and the kind of dynamics that would otherwise make board members and executives decide not to bring up or challenge difficult subjects.

In the Digital Age, boards have a special responsibility toward combating the outdated mantra, "Don't bring me a problem without a solution." Rather, you should cultivate candor by having executives and management teams bring forward the issues they are working on solving in the spirit of "what problems have we identified that need solving?"

Candor also makes it possible to evaluate performance more objectively. Most businesses experience turbulence and cyclicality, or, in other words, occasional head- and tailwind. What boards need to be obsessed about when it comes to both performance and transformation is to neutralize those effects and understand whether the company is actually "getting better at biking," more so than how fast they are driving at any given point in time.

Only by cultivating candor and building trust will boards be able to put in place the fundamentals for reinvention from a position of strength.

The cardinal sin when dealing with problems is to not offer or ask for help when needed.

The cardinal sin when dealing with problems should not be to point them out but to not offer or ask for help when needed. The board needs to ensure this is the approach throughout the organization by setting a tone from the top. In doing so, it can drive resilience, continuous improvement, and transformation throughout the organization.

Another important component critical to building outstanding performance dynamics in the boardroom is balance.

Getting the **balance** right is often proving particularly challenging.

Individual board members might have key competencies they like to promote, but when these turn into pet issues that are out of contextual balance with the overall agenda, it becomes counterproductive.

It is critical to keep discussions evolving around what is relevant to the opportunities and challenges the company is facing now and will face in the future. The same goes for ensuring there is more or less simultaneous focus on performance and transformation.

One way of accomplishing this is the simple meeting rule that "we discuss performance and results before lunch and transformation after lunch" and let the CEO determine when lunch is.

Discuss performance and results before lunch and transformation after lunch.

PERFORMANCE MANAGEMENT NEEDS TO BE REINVENTED . . .

As leaders, we know when results do not live up to our expectations. Our response has traditionally been to increase pressure on the organization to make even more precise goals and refine metrics to control the circumstances better. But the result will often be the opposite of what we want: we embed the company with the old season instead of driving it forward toward the next.

In a radically changing world, it is naive to think we can plan the future, and the problem with traditional management models is that they focus on executing and measuring what has been planned. They prioritize fulfilling the plan and do not evaluate whether the plan is still relevant.

When companies measure their revenue against a budget, it can give them an understanding of how well they have planned—but not how the market may change and who future competitors may be. An objective of achieving a 15 percent profit margin can be reached by cutting costs, but it could undermine the company's ability to grow in the future if it is done the wrong way. Also, 15 percent may turn out to be unambitious if new possibilities unexpectedly arise in the market and are not taken into account.

Changes of season will come more often in the future, and leaders must not only react to them but actively seek them out as opportunities.

Think back to 2007. Every provincial town had a Blockbuster video store. At the peak of the chain's popularity, it had almost 60,000 employees in about 9,000 stores in the United States.

If we were to predict the future back then, would we have guessed Blockbuster was facing a new season and would go bankrupt just ten years later, displaced by new digital competitors like Netflix? Hardly.

Netflix existed in 2007 but was not seen as a competitor at that time. In fact, Reed Hastings, cofounder and CEO of Netflix, had visited John Antioco, CEO of Blockbuster, in early 2000 with an offer to sell Netflix, which that year alone had lost $57 million, for $50 million. Just some 20 years later, Netflix was worth more than $200 billion.

Today, we talk a lot about disruption, the idea that new technologies and business models completely outcompete old businesses and approaches. However, the full scope of these changes and the speed by which they happen is often underestimated in big, successful companies.

The full scope of changes and the speed by which they happen is often underestimated.

Everything might seem solid—just like it did for Blockbuster. The bottom line results are fine, market share is often impressive, but the apparent success hides a crisis. Many companies struggle to continue their growth and remain market leaders for long periods.

Management does what they have done successfully for decades: create visions, missions, business plans, and budgets; set financial targets; define KPIs; and look at market shares. They do all the right things, according to what they have learned and what has worked successfully in the past.

Those methods have delivered returns year after year in the past. But instead of increasing growth and productivity, many companies now experience stagnant growth or even decline in revenue, and, as a result, they cut costs to protect profit.

It is not the employees' or managers' fault. What has changed are the circumstances—the market conditions and customer expectations. The problem is that plans are often developed based on historic experiences and data, and therefore they are only partly relevant for the future. The more uncertain the circumstances seem, the lower we define ambition level. Otherwise the plans seem unrealistic. As a result, the plans will not drive the needed change.

You cannot plan for an unpredictable future.

The methods we learned and used were developed at a time when the future was more predictable and where change happened slowly, giving us time to adjust. But you cannot plan for an unpredictable future, which is why our traditional management methods are less effective today, and in many cases, devastating to our ability to react to rapid change. Just ask Blockbuster, Kodak, and Nokia.

The Cranet Project is a global research project that examines and evaluates the results of different management methods. The project is the biggest and most comprehensive independent study of management policies and practices in the world. They examine organizations with more than a hundred employees in both the public and private sectors. The resulting data is unique because they offer an insight into what methods yield bottom line results.

According to the Cranet study, there is no evidence that performance management has an effect. There is no correlation between a company's results and the use of appraisal systems. The same can be said about many bonus systems and a number of other performance management methods.

Deloitte likewise surveyed global business leaders in their Global Human Capital Trends 2015 report and found widespread weariness of that kind of leadership. Only 8 percent of leaders said that performance management significantly improved results. Another 58 percent said that it is inefficient. According to Deloitte's report, the traditional performance management is damaging to employee engagement, alienates the best performers and consumes precious time.

It is time to use alternative forms of management systems and try new methods.

We still have to measure, follow-up and understand levels of performance and transformation. But incremental budgets supported by detailed business plans are insufficient and lacking agility in a radically changing world.

And even though we cannot plan the future, we can still arrive safely and well positioned.

Our Dreams & Details leadership model is all about inspiring and developing people to create the best opportunities for a successful reinvention of a company.

Dreams and details. You need both.

Dreams and details. You need both. Neither can stand alone. As the model below shows, it is a dynamic relationship where the direction, ambition, and inspiration of the dream determine which crucial details should have priority. But the opposite is also true: when roles, skills, and collaboration reach new levels, a new dream can be inspired. What seemed out of reach may now be possible to aim for. Add to that the platform of mindset and framework of the company that aim to minimize barriers and accelerate performance.

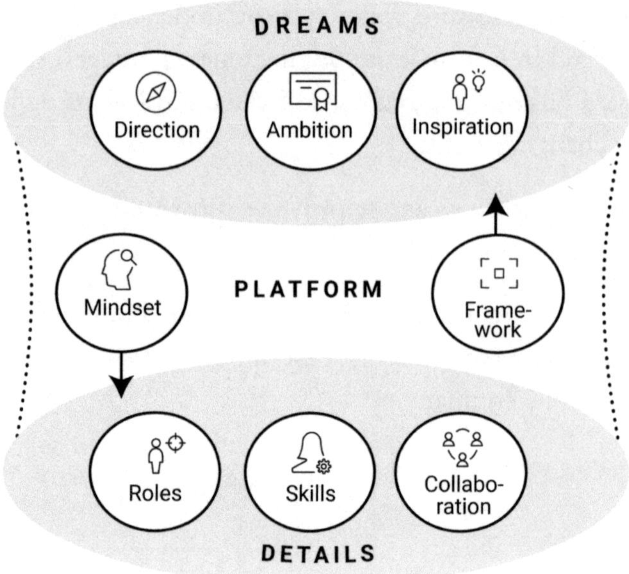

Figure 7 – Dreams & Details

When leaders develop a **dream** for the organization to pursue that is clear in its direction while being ambitious and inspiring for the whole organization, employees will see their work as meaningful and full of purpose. These are the key ingredients to real motivation and engagement.

Simultaneously, it will not limit the organization to specific predetermined results but leaves room to actually reach the optimal results. It may seem contradictory, but by not focusing on predetermined results, you will actually be likely to achieve better results.

On top of that, developing an inspiring dream for the whole organization is prone to resonate with outside stakeholders as well.

When a business anchors the contribution to solving larger issues, it will experience far more interest, sympathy, and willingness to engage by potential customers, partners, and other stakeholders.

An inspiring dream for the whole organization is prone to also resonate with outside stakeholders.

The dream creates the inspiration that fuels the work on the details, and working on the details unleashes human potential to make the dream come true and reinvent the company when the timing is right.

Boards need to have particular focus on the **details,** which are crucial to develop and train to succeed in the future. Without these details, the dream will stay just a dream.

Leaders need to ensure employees develop the skills that are vital to reaching the organization's ambition.

Moreover, leaders should make sure everyone is put in a role to succeed and foster collaboration between individuals, teams, and departments for more far-reaching, optimized solutions. When those conditions are met, the roles, skills, and collaboration become indispensable elements for succeeding with the details.

Finally, to make employees more autonomous decision makers and solution finders, leaders have to define and communicate a valuable mindset. The mindset embodies the understanding of how to make the optimal decisions to drive the organization's transformation and will become a point of reference for every decision that needs to be made.

At the same time, employees need a framework of rules and norms, the **Rule Book** to work in, marking the boundaries of action.

Once the mindset and framework are in place and fully embraced by the whole organization, employees have the **platform** that makes it possible to move more autonomously, responsibly, and creatively within these confines. This enables more decentralized decision-making within an organization and thus far higher speed and innovation.

As a result, leaders will unleash the potential of their individual employees but on an even more collective level, maximizing the organizational potential and performance.

. . . AND FOCUS MUST BE ON THE TOUGH QUESTIONS AND ON CHALLENGING KEY ASSUMPTIONS . . .

Only when boards embrace this mindset will executives be able to drive not merely performance but transformation. A board that stays in the old season will hinder transformation by focusing on what is becoming increasingly irrelevant, adhering to old logics and positions and past stories of glory.

We live in times where being directionally right and exactly wrong holds a lot of merit. Merely reading the material and identifying a few mistakes holds little value, if any. Adding value in the boardroom today begins with challenging assumptions and asking the essential questions.

Adding value begins with challenging assumptions and asking the essential questions.

Nowhere is this more obvious and important that in the work with strategy.

To give an example, Elon Musk decided early that Tesla intellectual property should be available on an open platform, realizing how that would make Tesla even more relevant in the future—not exactly the common assumption or line of thinking at the time.

Strategy can no longer be dealt with at an annual strategy seminar; it needs to be debated and evaluated at every board session.

One way of accomplishing that is to split the formulation of strategy into three distinct scan, focus, and act sessions that are then repeated annually.

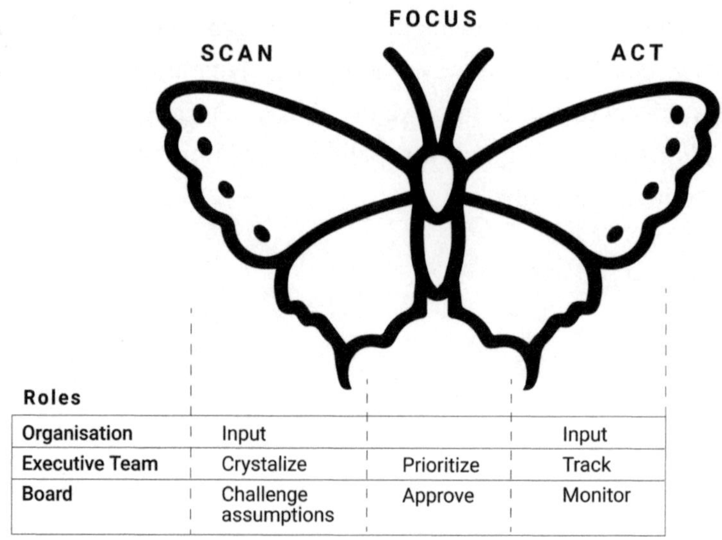

Roles			
Organisation	Input		Input
Executive Team	Crystalize	Prioritize	Track
Board	Challenge assumptions	Approve	Monitor

Figure 8 – Making Strategy Fly

The purpose of the scan phase is to ensure the board and executive team share all data that are relevant to understand the company's current situation, its pain points, and the trends expected to affect or disrupt it in the future. This **Situation Map** could just be a simple SWOT (Strengths, Weaknesses, Opportunities, Threats). The quality of the data is what matters and that it is sufficiently comprehensive. An added benefit of the Situation Map is that it can be revisited at every board meeting to keep an eye on issues and developments of strategic importance.

By having a shared picture of today, the board and the executive team are in a better position to consider what lies ahead and zoom in on the formulation of strategy.

Even though protecting and extracting value from the existing business is essential to having the resources to reinvent the business, it is important that the next phases of the strategy work does not get too deeply rooted in the current season.

The focus phase is all about spotting new seasons and painting pictures of the future.

The focus phase is all about spotting new seasons and painting pictures of the future.

The challenge is this: How do you best spot a new season? Which signs should you be looking for to realize that a season change is happening?

Start with a few simple questions:

- Which technologies are likely to change fundamentals in the industry, and how?

When you see a new competitor growing fast and acting differently, ask yourself,

- What are they doing differently?
- Which problem are they solving and how is their solution different?

If the reason for the high growth is that they are solving a relevant problem in a new way that customers appreciate, it is likely the beginning of a new season, in which case another question must be this:

- Do they provide customers something we cannot?

If the answer to that question is no, then ask yourself:

- What would it take for our company to do something similar—but at scale?

There is a risk that companies see their business and therefore competition too narrowly. Appreciating the full value chain in which a company operates is critical to strategy formulation.

Appreciating the full value chain in which a company operates is critical.

To get that thinking going, it might be useful to illustrate on a single sheet of paper the value chain and quantify its respective revenue and profit pools now on one side and in the future on the other.

The illustration on the next page is a description of the global transport and logistics value chain.

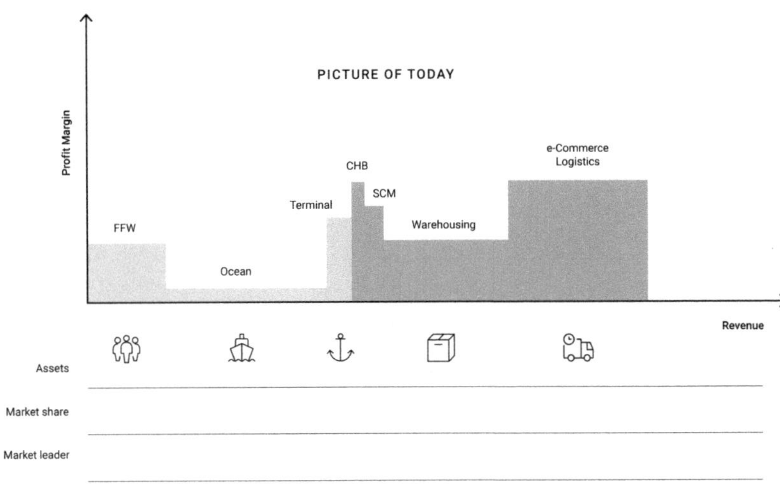

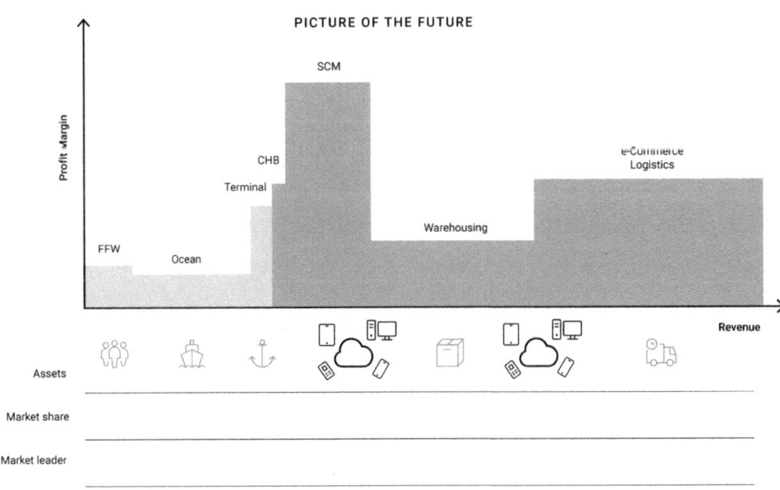

Figure 9 – Value Map

As figure 9 shows, the expectations are that the role of the freight forwarder will decrease while e-commerce and supply chain management will be the largest growth segments. Ocean shipping will not grow as a revenue pool, but consolidation will make it somewhat more profitable; however, it is still lacking supply chain, warehousing, and e-commerce, which are furthermore likely to become three times larger revenue pools.

Based on the **Value Map**, discussions can focus on the different positions the company could pursue that could have very different outcomes and investment requirements.

This approach has the added benefit that it creates a shared understanding of the process and how to keep the strategic discussions alive and real.

. . . TO BETTER UNDERSTAND AND CASCADE THE NARRATIVE . . .

The next step is for the executive team to move on to the focus phase.

Again, a one-page illustration is the best way to create a shared understanding of the crucial details required to make that happen.

Figure 10 illustrates the strategic journey Maersk is undertaking. As can be seen, early experiments were initiated on decarbonizing global shipping, and development focus has increased on digital and logistics while ocean and terminals were recognized as important pillars to fund that journey.

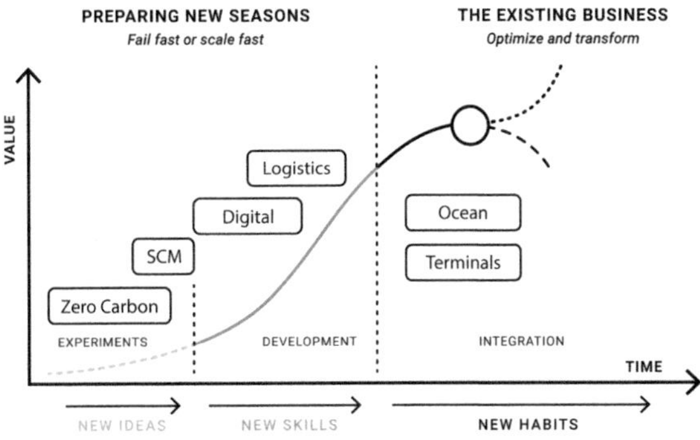

Figure 10 – Change of Season map

Having a shared strategy formulating approach and language will also make it far easier to cascade the strategy, which, after all, is the hard part.

Having a shared approach and language will make it far easier to cascade the strategy.

Crystalizing a shared understanding of the strategy, its focus and priorities is critical. To make that happen, you need a **Play Book**. The Play Book summarizes where the company plays (Situation and Value Maps), and what the transformation will entail (Change of Season Map). Together, these maps outline the rationale for the strategic journey ahead. But boards should challenge the executive team to also formulate the strategy on a single sheet of paper.

One way of doing that is the **Strategy Map**. The one below summarizes (in hindsight) SAP's strategy when it was formulated back in 2010.

Our DREAM is to . . .		. . . make the world run better – and improve peoples lives			
We want to . . .	Mindset	. . . reach 1 billion people with our solutions by 2015 (from 50 million in 2010)			
Our ambition is to . . .	Ambition	. . . double revenue to EUR 20 billion within 5 years . . .		. . . and be the fastest growing company in new markets	
We achieve that by . . .	Inspiration	. . . leveraging our core in managing resources for companies to manage scarce resources across entire vaue chains			
The coming years we focus on . . .	Direction	. . . defending our leadership positions in ERP and 3 new markets . . .		Mobile technology Big data/In-memory database Cloud-based solutions	
We need to get some crucial DETAILS right ...		. . . double the speed of innovation (from 15 months to 6) and . . .		. . . be obsessed with customer success (increase "share of wallet" from 5% to 10%)	
and work in new ways . . .	Frame-work	From hierarchal to self-managed teams	From "Waterfall" to "Agile"	From R&D to platform-based R&D	
take on new roles . . .	Roles	Product owners	Scrum masters	Key account	Customer support
develop new skills . . .	Skills	Simplicity	Usability	Cloud	M&A
and collaborate in new ways	Colla-boration	Agile	LEAN principles		UI first

All based on living our shared values . . .			
. . . Leadership principles			
. . . and workplace attitudes			

Figure 11 – Strategy Map

Being able to illustrate the strategy on a single page and being able to explain it during the time it takes to ride the elevator is vital. Having a shared approach and language will make it far easier to cascade the strategy.

It is not an easy task. As Winston Churchill once pointed out, "If you want me to speak for two minutes, it will take me three weeks of preparation. If you want me to speak for thirty minutes, it will take me a week to prepare. If you want me to speak for an hour, I am ready now."

As visualized, the Strategy Map can also be used to reiterate company values, leadership principles, and workplace attitudes. As Peter Drucker, management consultant, observed, "Culture eats strategy for breakfast." Warren Buffett, one of the most successful investors of our time, later added. "Every day."

Culture is the character and spirit of the company.

Culture is the character and spirit of the company. It is what personifies its brand. A brand is a promise, so when it comes to culture, obviously a lot is at stake, and it is critical that the board sees itself as the guardian of company culture, which comprises three components:

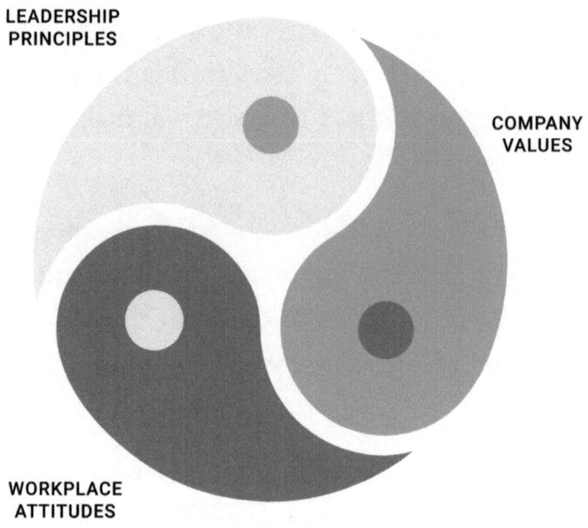

Figure 12 – Culture

- Values – Which all employees and the board must radiate
- Leadership Principles – Which all with leadership responsibilities must rolemodel to drive performance and transformation
- Workplace attitudes – Which all employees must embrace to create psychological safety and an inclusive atmosphere that can attract the best

Being the guardian of company culture is no trivial task. Be careful you do not confuse guardian with custodian. Sometimes a company culture needs to change for the company to transform. As guardians, the board needs to recognize when this is the case to help drive the necessary change rather than preserving something that is holding the potential of the company back.

. . . AND DEFINE THE METRICS CRITICAL TO WINNING THE NEXT SEASON.

Apart from enabling and enforcing culture one of the most potent powers the board holds is to determine how success is defined and measured. This is what the act phase is all about. It includes preparing the Performance and Transformation Books, which allows focus on both winning this season and positioning the company for the next.

Traditionally this has been inseparable from financial results, but when you pursue and drive transformation to redefine this as an opportunity not to be missed. There should be no doubt in the organization as to “how we do things around here” or “what it takes to succeed.”

Financial measures are lagging by nature, and in recognition of that, most companies have complemented their Key Performance Indicators with some more leading operational key figures. But that is not sufficient. Indicators are also needed to measure transformational pace.

At SAP in 2009, success was defined by more than 5,000 targets in the company. The KPIs were used to measure how different departments were performing against defined business plans. Each department had decided on three to five KPIs to describe their contribution to the overall plan for the company. Each department would pay a bonus based on the achievement of the individual targets.

How do you focus on the new opportunities in the next season when most employees are measured by the logic of the old season?

With more than 45,000 employees, perhaps it makes sense that individual employees are held responsible for three to five measurable goals. However, what is the possibility that all employees in the company will head in the same direction when they are measured on 5,000 different objectives? How do you ensure there is sufficient focus on the new opportunities in the next season when most employees are measured by the logic of the old season? How do you avoid a situation in which most individual goals are met but the company still becomes irrelevant because it is just optimizing the past, not reinventing for the future?

It is important to understand another aspect of the digital development: it has made the world more transparent. We can connect instantly and share massive amounts of data constantly; we are connected nearly everywhere and can keep up with changes in real time. This means employees in a company often have better and more detailed knowledge of, for instance, customer expectations, changes in the competitive landscape, and new competitors than top management.

> Employees are often the first to notice a change of season.

Traditionally, the big picture was reserved for management, but today employees have access to a lot of very detailed information, and, thanks to social media, they can monitor how consumers react to products and services. Employees are often the first to notice a change of season, but they may be measured and rewarded not according to their ability to point it out but to follow the logic in the old season. They may suggest doing something new, but it will often interfere with the performance goals set for themselves and others. In short, employees are limited by how they are measured. It is essential that the way we measure the company's performance, its leaders, and employees supports the company's strategy. That counts for the current season but is even more critical when it comes to experimenting, developing, and getting ready for the next season. If not, we increase the risk of rising meaninglessness and declining motivation and engagement.

One way of ensuring that is the formulation of Performance and Transformation Books that consist of each business unit's and department's description of what great looks like now and in the future.

It need not be more than a single sheet of paper for each, but it needs to clearly outline how you measure the individual business unit's and department's performance now and define the measures that will be critical in the future as well as what crucial initiatives they need to work on and train in order to drive both.

By focusing business units and departments on what it takes to both win the races of this season **(Performance Book)**, and preparing for the next **(Transformation Book)** companies also ensure that all share and work on the same dream. And that the focus of its departments and business units is on what it takes to get there.

Once the performance and transformation initiatives have been established, they can be plotted into a **Focus Map** that helps especially the board ensure it spends sufficient time with the executive team, discussing initiatives that are crucial to the impact and success of the transformation and with which the company might not historically have had a lot of experience and expertise with. Training those muscles is particularly important.

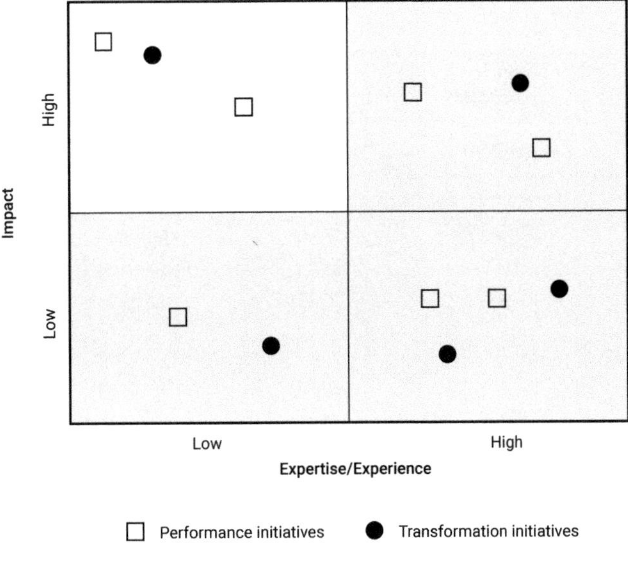

Figure 13 – Focus Map

The benefit of this matrix is that it allows members of the board and executive team to agree on which initiatives have the largest impact on performance now and in the future and where the organization has relative strong and weak capabilities in that context. For areas with little experience the board should encourage a more experimental approach, where the focus is to learn, whereas for areas with lots of experience in the company, the board can delegate more and ask for updates on progress.

That way it becomes much easier to reach alignment on prioritizing what should be in focus, avoiding that too much time is spent on issues that were important in the old season but which have since become less relevant.

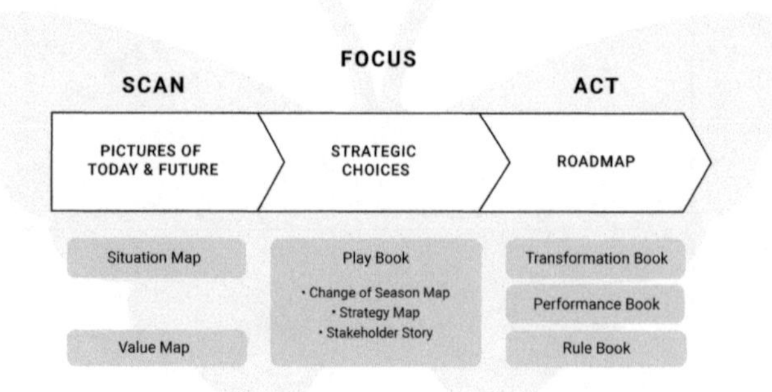

Figure 14 – Strategy work in times of radical change

Boards need to have the curiosity not least to insist on occasional deep-dives into the Transformation Book to ensure solid performance comes hand in hand with solid progress on the crucial details for the future.

> Boards need to have the curiosity to insist on occasional deep-dives into the Transformation Book.

Getting key stakeholders along on the journey is critical, and so is being ready to deal with crisis.

Chapter 3

BOARDS ENABLE EXECUTION OF STRATEGY BY GETTING THE RIGHT TEAM IN PLACE ...

To succeed, it is increasingly important to have strong individuals on the teams who have the competencies required to succeed in the future and understand and buy into both the Rule and Play Books.

Once it has been decided how to play the game in the future, you have to evaluate whether you have the team in place to lead that reinvention.

Frequent assesment of the executives should be made. Having the right competencies is critical to reinvention. Creating talent for the future is critical to unleash the company's full potential.

At INSEAD's AVIRA program, one of the modules is about what it takes to be a dream team.

A group is defined by a shared dream, rules, and goal, and it is bound by trust in one another.

To perform as a team, you need furthermore to have clearly agreed-upon roles, a shared motivation, and focus on talent development.

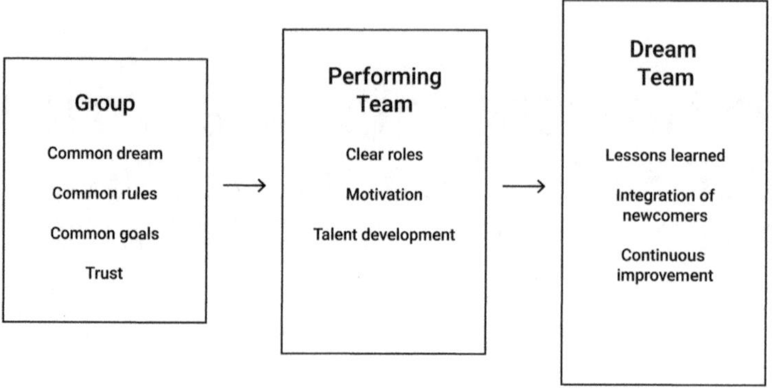

Figure 15 – Dream Team

It furthermore requires effective integration of newcomers as well as a mindset characterized by lessons learned and continuous improvement to perform as a Dream Team.

It is worthwhile as a board to conduct sanity checks once in a while and definitely at the board seminar to ensure that these components are all well in place. When they are, valuable momentum and unity within the executive team is built.

With people increasingly being the real differentiator and uniqueness of companies, expanding leadership capacity must be a focus area also for the board. And developing leadership and not just choosing leaders has a few important added benefits:

- Lower risk: Outside executives are more likely to have mismatching prior experience and lack the internal social networks and connections, which can hamper their effectiveness.
- More cost effective: The executive remuneration explosion of recent years has been driven in no small part by a lack of inside leadership development. In the world of sports, developing leadership is an integrated approach that is an important source to value creation. Companies must embrace a similar mindset.

Naturally, it is important that companies also benefit from external talent at every level of the organization, however, it would seem a sensible target that two-thirds of leadership promotions are made among colleagues who are already employed in the company. When it is considered a liability to work in the company already, there is a risk that the best talent will start looking elsewhere for opportunities to grow and develop.

If in three years you have not developed a successor, then you leave.

A practical way to drive leadership expansion is the **Succession Map** and a mindset that "if in three years you have not developed a successor, then you leave."

Just a single sheet for Tier 2 and each of their teams will quickly give the board an impression of the solidity of the leadership pipeline and that it has the competencies to perform both now and in the future.

Succession Map	Name	Name	Name	Name	Name	Name
Role						
With company since						
In current role since						
Performance						
Potential						
Criticality of position						
Experience with current season						
Experience with next season						
In-house successors now						
In-house successors +2Y						
External candidates						

Figure 16 – Succession Map

. . . WITH THE RIGHT INCENTIVES.

Related to the task of defining the right performance and transformation metrics, the board or remuneration committee has the responsibility to establish the right incentive structure.

This work is not just a matter of determining the level of remuneration but more importantly about determining what success looks like.

It is likely that good executive teams will do what is best for the company rather than being affected by the components of the incentive plan. But even then, the board sets the tone about what it determines to be the right focus and the right balance between winning the current and future seasons.

Having transformational targets as part of the incentive reiterates the importance of preparing for the future.

GETTING KEY STAKEHOLDERS ALONG ON THE JOURNEY IS CRITICAL . . .

Korn Ferry found that 85 percent of CEOs interviewed for its "CEO's for the Future" say the boundaries between business and society are ever more porous. They recognize building sustainable, growing businesses for shareholders and engaging employees also requires increasing attention to communities and the environment.

It is no longer sufficient to do no harm.

The old mantra "the business of business is business" needs to be abandoned. It is no longer sufficient to do no harm. Business leaders are expected to be courageous and do the right things and be part of a change for the better.

Stakeholder capitalism is a system in which corporations are oriented to serve the interests of all their stakeholders as opposed to just maximizing shareholder value (MSV), which coincidentally Jack Welch, a previous CEO of General Electric, called back in 2009 "the dumbest idea in the world." More diplomatically, Harvard Business School Professor Joseph L. Bower, already denounced MSV when it was launched by Milton Friedman back in 1970 as "pernicious nonsense."

Stakeholder capitalism was the theme of the Davos Manifesto 2020 and is the title of a book that Klaus Schwab, the founder and executive chair of the World Economic Forum, released in 2021.

In many ways, this is what could be called enlightened self-interest. Even skeptics of stakeholder capitalism seem to agree that business must ultimately pay attention to all its stakeholders and that if businesses systematically shortchange stakeholders rather than shareholders, the stock may soar in the short term but for a variety of reasons (customer abandonment, regulation, etc.) suffer in the long term.

Companies that fail to embrace stakeholder capitalism will also find it increasingly difficult to attract talent and cost effective capital. Companies that focus on multiple bottom lines experience that it is not just the right thing to do, it is also good business.

> Companies that focus on multiple bottom lines experience that it is good business.

The renewable energy sector is a good example. A subsidized energy source just a few years ago, wind is today the second most cost-effective electricity source. The most cost-effective is solar, which also just a few years ago was a subsidized energy source.

Both technologies benefited from effective scale up that made it possible to reduce unit costs to levels unimaginable just years earlier.

Biogas is next, and the same will happen to renewable fuels like methanol and ammonia, which are set to benefit from Power-to(-Hydrogen-to)-X opportunities made possible by the low-cost renewable energy sources. Soon we will be able to make shipping and land-based transportation zero emission and possibly even also a big part of aviation.

A common denominator for these is the urgency brought on by climate change.

Skeptics claim we cannot afford to mitigate and stop climate change, and the fact is that decarbonizing transportation of goods which accounts for 9 percent of global carbon dioxide emission is likely to cost $2 trillion and increase fuel costs by a factor of two to three times with current technology.

The price of these fuels is bound to come down as facilities to produce them are scaled, however. But even at these prices, a pair of sneakers transported from Asia to the US or Europe would only cost $.05 more than they do today. And while $2 trillion is a lot of money, it is actually the equivalent to just four years of capital expenditure in the oil and gas sector.

Similar scenarios are bound to drive other industries and sectors, and, as Tony Seba reminded us, this will ultimately affect all businesses. And bring all of us a more sustainable future.

The board should challenge the executive team to formulate a Stakeholder Story.

Just like the board should challenge the executive team to crystalize the strategy on a single page, it should also challenge the team to formulate a **Stakeholder Story**.

Anyone actively involved in private equity and Mergers & Acquisitions will be very familiar with the importance of equity stories and full potential plans. The benefit of these are that they spell out the compelling reasons to invest in a business. Even if you have been the owner of a business for years and have no plans to sell it, this practise is a good discipline that forces all to crystalize the essence and quantify what great looks like.

Boards should move beyond that and insist that the conclusion of any strategy process should be the formulation of Stakeholder Story as opposed to merely an equity story. A Stakeholder Story should include—as a minimum and in addition to the investor perspective—the reason the best talent should work for the company and how the company plans to add value to society at large.

We would also argue that including this perspective brings upside to any full potential plan, at least in the medium and long term, because a business in tune and aligned with the megatrends and societal expectations is bound to fair better and be more investable.

The focus on sustainability has already contributed to making stakeholder management more complicated for most companies.

Getting all shareholders on such journeys can be a challenge—especially those whose investment is limited to weeks or months, or sometimes even just a few seconds, or those who subscribe to Clayton Christensen's innovator dilemma and seem to believe that transformation is about them moving investments between old and new companies.

Performance is the license to transformations. But by focusing only on the former, such shareholders actually risk systemizing the status quo just like poorly designed incentive structures do.

Restrictive covenants, while perfectly understandable, ironically risk doing the same.

Performance is the license to transformations.

This was also the case at SAP when the decision was taken to move away from a software model, which was delivering record-high earnings, to a cloud-based license business.

Initially the share price suffered but only to recover and bring SAP and its shareholders onto the next sigmoid curve. Years later, the share price of SAP suffered because the move to the cloud was too slow—a strong indicator that the new season in business software was in full motion.

For the executive team, to be able to focus on both the performance and transformation of the company, it is critical that the stakeholder story is effectively and widely communicated.

. . . AND SO IS BEING READY TO DEAL WITH CRISIS.

Most companies have extensive risk evaluations, and although these probably did not predict the Icelandic ash cloud or the COVID-19 pandemic, they are by and large good input for the strategy work and also a good discipline for proactive mitigation work of pain points.

Understand the difference between an incident and a crisis.

Companies often fail to understand the difference between an incident and a crisis. Confusing them can be detrimental.

For some reason, boards and executives seem too often to fail to understand the gravity of these situations and are poorly prepared to effectively handle issues like these.

Perhaps because communication skills are rarely seen as a key competence in a board, or because the board has a limited understanding of how fast a situation can escalate from incident, if it is not handled well, to full blown crisis, thanks not least to social media. Many boards have been used to thinking about shareholders, but as mentioned previously today stakeholders are at least as important. Poor conduct in relation to for instance diversity, environment or discrimination can quickly become a financial problem as well and have negative impact on the license to operate.

One helpful framework for dealing with a crisis is to recognize that not all crises can be prevented but that mitigation measures can still be taken and activities and actions can be prepared that improve the ability to respond and recover.

CRISIS MANAGEMENT				
Prevention	Mitigation	Preparedness	Response	Recovery
Actions taken to avoid an incident	Measures that can prevent an emergency and reduce damage	Activities that improves the ability to respond	Actions carried out immediately before, during, and after an impact	Actions taken to restore to (near) normal conditions

Figure 17 – Crisis Management

In times of crisis, the board and chair tend to get involved swiftly, and at that stage it is often too late to prepare.

Putting the risk matrix into crisis management use and understanding the issues from a stakeholder perspective is critical to effectively handle crisis.

At stake is the reputation of the company, which, next to culture, is one of the guardian responsibilities the board has.

The reputation of the company is a guardian responsibility of the board.

MOMENTUM DEPENDS ON THE UNITY BETWEEN BOARDS AND EXECUTIVES . . .

Apart from the relations with its stakeholders, another key relationship that needs to be strong is the one between the chair and the CEO.

The chair, apart from being the day-to-day link between the owners and the CEO, is also the one to keep the rest of the board informed between ordinary meetings.

Not only does this balancing act demand a significant time commitment, it also takes virtuous leadership capabilities.

Just like *Aufsichsrat* seems more relevant than "board," it might also be time to reconsider "chair," which after all merely is a historic reference to the one person of authority who sat in a chair hundreds of years ago while everyone else was standing around the table.

"Conductor" might be the better description of the skills that this person is expected to add to a competent room of board members and executives.

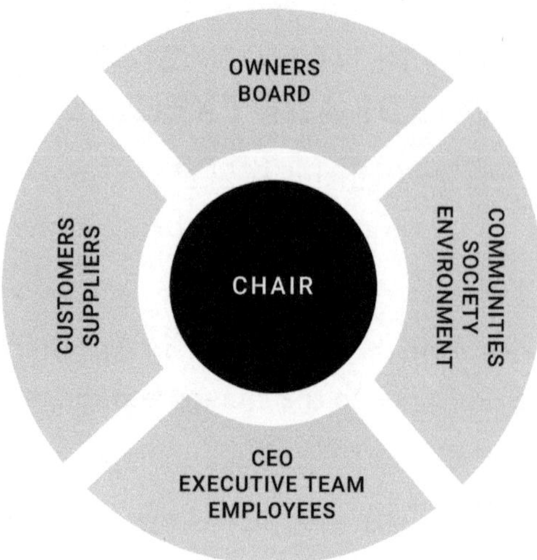

Figure 18 – Chair Stakeholders

Benjamin Zander, conductor of the Boston Philharmonic Orchestra, in his master/interpretation classes, will inspire to a type of uncompromising yet caring type of leadership.

Virtuous leadership by the chair can also beneficially be modeled on the research by Stanislaw Shekshnia, professor at INSEAD, who presented his findings in the Harvard Business Review article *How to Be a Good Board Chair* based on research by INSEAD's Corporate Governance Center, which conducted a survey of 200 board chairs from thirty-one countries, and held interviews with eighty chairs and sixty board members, shareholders, and CEOs.

Despite some contextual differences (mostly related to ownership structure and, to a lesser extent, national culture), they found a remarkable degree of agreement about what makes a good chair.

A common theme was that an effective chair provides leadership not to the company but to the board.

Herman Daems, chair of BNP Paris Fortis, taught at Harvard Business School and IESE Business School. He has made similar observations in his book *Insights from the Boardroom,* in which he presents what he calls the "duty diamond" and defines the respective roles of the board and chair.

BOARD		
DUTIES	ROLES	
	Board	Chair
Setting the course	• Ensuring the right management • Ensuring an effective strategy	• Knowing key staff
Supervision and monitoring	• Ensuring the availablity and proper use of resources	• Organize corporate governance • Last resort for whistleblowers • Having a feel for timing
Setting standards and promulgating values		• Promoting in-depth deliberations
Accountability	• Assuming responsibility	• Taking the initiative if things go wrong
		• Ensuring the board is able to carry out its functions and is, and remains, able to make decisions • Contact with shareholders • Contact with and appraisal of directors

Figure 19 – Duties and Roles

When it comes to organizing the corporate governance part of the board agenda, it is essential that the chair makes use of a solid committee structure but also plans and handles these issues so they do not take up unnecessary time at the meetings. As mentioned earlier, governance cannot be allowed to be the only subject. Performance has to be paired with transformation at every meeting.

Although the chair handles most of the interaction with the executive team, all board members need to be conscious of how important they are in creating a strong sense of unity between the board and the executive team.

All board members need to be conscious of how important they are in creating a strong sense of unity between the board and the executive team.

One way of aligning the board with the CEO is to include a board seminar with that purpose in the annual wheel. At the seminar board members and the CEO can align on:

- Competencies: Critical insights into both this season and the next
- Style: The understanding of how the board adds value and the traits which must characterize its approach

- Focus: Determining the perform / transform balance by using the Focus Map.

... AND THE SPACE AND ENERGY CREATED TO UNLEASH THE FULL POTENTIAL.

Momentum is also gained when the board is conscious of how it can contribute energy to the increasingly hectic everyday life of executives and employees.

It has become good practice at the end of every board meeting that the board quickly assesses how the meeting went and whether adjustments to the annual wheel are required.

It should be equally common that, after every meeting, the board asks itself these key questions:

- Did we focus on the right things?
- Did we have candid and constructive discussions resulting in better decisions?
- Did we prioritize and make it easier to perform and transform?
- Did we add energy and enthusiasm?

Chapter 4

RECOMMENDATIONS

Checklists for Making Strategy Fly

As a checklist, we have summarized a set of essential questions relative to each of the maps and books that facilitate the board's work with developing, formulating, and monitoring strategy.

Situation Map	
Checklist	**Status**
• How dependent are we of individual clients?	☐
• How resilient are our supply chains?	☐
• How are we performing relative to competition?	☐
• How will megatrends affect us in the coming years?	☐
• How solid is our liquidity and capital structure, and how significant is our investment capacity?	☐
• What are our worst pain points and the most catastrophic risks we face?	☐
• What are our greatest opportunities?	☐
• How solid is our talent pipeline?	☐
• How robust is our succession plan?	☐

Value Map	
Checklist	**Status**
• Which value chain are we part of?	☐
• Which revenue and profit pools does that value chain comprise?	☐
• What are our fundamental beliefs about how our value chain is likely to develop in the years to come?	☐

Strategy Map	
Checklist	**Status**
• What dream are we pursuing?	☐
• What will be our direction the coming years?	☐
• What is our ambition?	☐
• To get there, which mindset and inspiration must guide us?	☐
• What are the crucial details we need to get right the coming years?	☐
• What framework, roles, skills and ways of cooperation are required to effectively deliver on our strategy?	☐
• What will characterize the culture of the company and its leadership?	☐

Stakeholder Story

Checklist	Status
• What are our unique value propositions to our various stakeholders?	☐
• How do we add value to society at large?	☐
• What does full potential look like?	☐

Performance Book

Checklist	Status
• What does great look like in this season?	☐
• Where are we doing well and where do we need to improve further?	☐

Transformation Book

Checklist	Status
• What metrics will be critical to win the next season?	☐
• Which new competencies and skills do we need to develop and train?	☐

We need to recognize that many businesses have become more global and powerful than even some nations. As leaders of companies, we have a special obligation in times like these.

CALL TO ACTION

We live in special times or, as Charles Dickens wrote, "It was the best of times, it was the worst of times."

It is easy to despair, but underneath its sinister surface and the disruptions we all face, there is plenty to take courage from.

There is nothing new about having to adapt to change. What is new is the pace with which change happens and the simultaneous and radical nature of the changes we are witnessing. However, once again, humans proved during COVID-19 that we are capable of changing and adjusting.

We are the only known species with the gift of imagination and the ability to communicate our dreams and aspirations.

Let us radiate that spirit from boardrooms around the world and thus make our individual contributions to a better world with purposeful jobs and the opportunity to prosper for generations to come.

The old way was not wrong—but it eventually will be. We are rapidly approaching the inflection point for leadership where we need to put a few old habits and mantras behind us and replace them with new traits and a new mindset.

The political landscape is also under pressure from technological advances which challenge what we have so far known to be facts and the truth.

As a result, politicians have a harder and harder time doing what is right for the long term and cannot solve issues on their own.

We need to recognize that many businesses have become more global and powerful than even some nations. As leaders of companies, we have a special obligation in times like these. Luckily, we also have better opportunities than ever to make it happen.

President John F. Kennedy launched his moon project, which brought along a significant number of technological breakthroughs and changed the trajectory of geopolitics at the time.

With the UN Sustainable Development Goals adopted at the 2015 Summit, we have seventeen such projects all in urgent need of getting tackled.

This is a leadership moment.

Jesper, Jim, and Mikael

ABOUT THE AUTHORS

Jesper Lok is Vice-Chair at Idonea. From 1987 to 2004, Jesper held a variety of leadership positions at Maersk in Japan, Taiwan, Pakistan, and Nigeria. After that, he was CEO of the Maersk division SVITZER for eight years and CEO of DSB (Danish Passenger Railroads) during its transformation from 2012 to 2014. Since 2014, Jesper has focused on board work, including Dagrofa, G&O, Nature Energy, Inchcape, Vestergaard, and UNICEF. Jesper holds an MBA and has attended a range of business schools in Asia, Europe, and North America.

Jim Hagemann Snabe is Chair at Idonea and Chair of Siemens AG (D), former Chair of A.P. Møller – Maersk A/S (DK), and former Vice-Chair of Allianz SE (D). He is a board member of C3.ai, and a member of the board of trustees at World Economic Forum. Jim has developed his career through 25 years of service in the IT industry. Throughout his career, Jim has had leadership roles at SAP and IBM, leading global consulting, sales and product development organizations. He was appointed member of the executive board of SAP in 2008 and co-CEO of SAP AG in 2010 alongside Bill McDermott. Through his involvement with the World Economic Forum, Jim is actively engaged in efforts related to the digital transformation of business and society. Jim has an MSc (Economics and Business Administration) from Aarhus University and is adjunct professor at Copenhagen Business School.

Mikael Trolle is the CEO and Partner of Idonea and cowriter of the book *Dreams & Details—Reinvent Your Business From a Position of Strength*. For 28 years, he was CEO and sports director in Volleyball Denmark and for two periods, the head coach of the men's national volleyball team. Mikael's career has spanned eight years as an international volleyball player followed by twenty-one years in head coaching positions at club and international level, summing up 342 matches spearheading the men's national team. He is a lecturer and examiner at the University of Copenhagen and Copenhagen Business School. As a consultant and corporate advisor, he has worked with numerous Danish and international companies and organizations, such as Novo Nordisk, The Danish Government, The Royal Danish Theater, and the Danish Broadcasting Corporation DR. Mikael holds an MSc in Biology and Sports Science from the University of Copenhagen.

INDEX